ETHICS AND PEOPLE'S ISSUES

Books by the Same Author

- **Human Rights:** Concepts and Perspectives (2002)
- **Christian Ethics:** Issues and Insights (2007)
- **Contextual Issues:** Theological, Ethical and Missiological Responses (2011)
- **Introducing Post Modernism and Post Colonialism** (2013)
- **Post Colonialism Subalterns and Community** (2015)
- **Ethics and the Community of God** (2022)

About the Author

Rev. Dr M. Stephen hails from Kottayam (Kerala, India) is a writer, orator and author. He has authored around 30 books in Malayalam and English. He received his BA and MA (in English Literature) from Kerala University, BD (UBS, Pune) and MTh (UTC, Bangalore) from Serampore University (West Bengal), and Doctorate from Dharmaram Vidyakshetram: Pontificial Athenaeum of Philosophy and Theology, Bangalore. He is a theological teacher and teaches theology and ethics at Faith Theological Seminary, Manakala, Adoor, Kerala. The famous publishers such as "Concept", "Serials" and ISPCK have published his books. *Human Rights, Contextual Issues, Christian Ethics: Issues and Insights*, and *Introducing Post-modernism and Post-colonialism* are published by Concept Publishing Company Pvt. Ltd., Delhi.

ETHICS AND PEOPLE'S ISSUES

M. Stephen

CONCEPT PUBLISHING COMPANY PVT. LTD.
NEW DELHI - 110 059

ISBN: 978-93-5594-873-1

First Published 2024

Published and Printed by

Concept Since 1974

Concept Publishing Company Pvt. Ltd.
A/15-16, Commercial Block, Mohan Garden
New Delhi-110059 (India)
T: +91-11-41101460
E: publishing@conceptpub.com, *W*: www.conceptpub.com

Cataloging in Publication--Courtesy: D.K. Agencies (P) Ltd. <docinfo@dkagencies.com>

Sṯīphan, Em̦., author.
Ethics and people's issues / M. Stephen.
pages cm
Includes bibliographical references and index.
ISBN 9789355948731

1. Social ethics--India. 2. Social problems--India. 3. Political ethics--India. 4. India--Politics and government--21st century. I. Title.

LCC HN683.5.S78 2024 | DDC 303.3720954 23

Introduction

Ethics and People's Issues deals with various issues of the people from different social contexts. This include the subaltern communities, the minorities, ethnic groups, and people with psychological issues. The issues related to development, fascism, pseudo-secularism, ethnic crises, the Farmers Bill, Uniform Civil Code, the war, human sexuality, concept of *dharma* and political rule are discussed in this book.

It explores the nature of development that does not take care of the integral liberation of the subaltern communities. What is going on in the name of development is very lopsided and attending the comforts of the elites. The struggle of the ethnic groups and minority communities in the context of pseudo-secularism is another issue where their identity and security are being challenged. There are also the crises like war, especially Russian–Ukraine conflict which did harm the life of the people in both countries, especially it had very adversely affected the Ukranians. This is also true with Israel–Palestinian conflict. The Farmers Bill in India also was a serious question for the Indian farmers and there was an organized protest against it and at last the Bill was withdrawn by the authorities.

The issues like the sanctitiy of sex is also discussed as there are distorted understanding on sexuality. The ethical concerns in the context of counselling, that is, the role of ethics in counselling is also discussed. The minorities and ethnic groups are also undergoing life threatening situation because of victimization and the violent attacks. It is also a question whether the minorities are safe or secularism will prevail under the Hindutva ideology and pseudo-secularism. There is also the suppression of the social media which discloses the real fact. Hindutva agenda is implemented, but regret to say that the people's issues are disregarded. This is the ethical dilemma in the Indian context. It is very important to explore, what would be the nature of India in the future?

This book provides some studies and reflections on complex issues that people face in the context. Hope this insights may be eye-openers for our further explorations.

M. Stephen

Contents

Chapter
1

Development and the Subaltern Communities

Introduction

It is very significant to have development for the welfare of the people. It should lead to the integral or wholistic progress and development. What is important is how the development programmes are positively affecting the people in general and especially the subaltern communities like the Dalits, tribes, the fisherfolk, slum dwellers, victimized women, children, LGBTIQA+ communities, the differently abled, the refugees and migrants. The most crucial issue is the development or socio-economic transformation of the powerless and voiceless people of India.

I. *Definitions, Perspectives and Insights on "Development" and "Subaltern"*

In this section, we are trying to define and understand the "development" and "subaltern".

(a) *The Perspective on Development*

Development is a modern concept, but there was progress in the world all through the centuries. Development is now associated to modernization. The concept was developed after the Second World War, as there was poverty and unemployment, and damage of the infrastructure. The then American President John F. Kennedy initiated the development and the United Nations declared a "development decade". The "development" is an overarching concept which includes spiritual and moral, socio-economic and political aspects.

The capitalists and corporates are trying to explain the development to mean profiteering. They have an eye on land and other resources beside their project or business. They have the benefit of profit in different ways. The globalization and the neo-liberal politics are tied up with capitalists and policies of the corporates. It is observed that before the First World War (1914) only 20 per cent of the total wealth was held by 1 per cent of the wealthy class, but today the wealthy class are holding more than 90 per cent of the wealth. This is the serious inequality that prevails. This means the majority income generating resources are in the hands of the rich.

According to the study of United Nations, though the world is in progress the inequality is at the increase. The first world is hundredfold rich compared to the Third World. The number of the rich are increasing so also the number of the poor. The malnutrition among the rural people increased from 54 to 68 per cent, and among urban people it is 57 to 65 per cent. Twenty crore people in the world are not getting drinking water.

The capitalists, corporates and other powerful forces are keen on controlling the resources which are income-generating. Acquiring the land, the seashores and the forests in order to tap the resources and to build-up their mega projects are the prime agenda of these forces. They are capital intensive and promote the free-trade or free-market economy. They use all means to make profit. The deforestation and the tapping of resources lead to descitification. It is to be noted that the industrialization of modern era has contributed to the global warming and the global climatic change. The utilization of the new technologies is also a powerful instrument for the capitalistic structures to accelerate their profit.

The globalization or neo-liberal politics like liberalization and privatization are the neo-colonial agenda of the Euro-centric capitalists and their Third World collaborators. The unholy nexus of the corporates have globalized the poverty. The rich becomes more rich and the poor became more poor. This is the consequence of globalization. The globalization has disempowered the poor and marginalized. The machinery has hijacked the skilled products of the poor. What is made by blacksmith, and the traditional skilled people are now made in the factories by the corporates and they control the market.

The reckless development and machanization have created unemployment and according to Pope Francis, "where there is no employment, there no dignity". The present economic order for God is moving to disaster. According to Pope Francis, the understanding of God is that the centre of our economic order should not be money but human being. The capitalists are deliberately skipping the values. They are after quick money and easy money. They are after the commodification of land, water, education and health. The author of *Wealth of Nations* Adam Smith argues that every economic system stands for competition and profit. Instead of profit, we can add that all profits are made through exploitation and oppression. These are the colonial and neo-colonial project. The "trickle down" theory also argues that the poor can come up, as the rich are becoming more rich. This perspective is supporting the idea that the poor have to live by collecting crumbs. Unless the basic necessities of the poor and marginalized are met, there is no way that they could come up in their status and dignity. That concept is only a mirage.

The overall growth of all sections of people is a significant concern in the concept of development, but it is so happened that only the powerful are reaching the top and controlling the resources and the poor are sidelined. The distribution of power and economic resources are not taking place in equitable terms. There are several development approaches like capitalist, political economy, United Nations, but the question is whether the development programmes are meeting the basic needs of the people, especially the powerless. When there is exploitation, injustice, corruption and inequality, it is very evident that there is no adequate development taking place.

The condition of the urban and rural poor is pathetic in Indian situation. They live in extreme poverty and underdeveloped situation. The urban poor live mostly in slums and streets and are undergoing hunger, shelterless situation and unemployment. They also suffer from scarcity of water and sanitation. Most of them fail to send their children to schools. In rural situation, the condition is worse as there is problem of extreme poverty, unemployment, lack of medical facilities, transportation, educational facilities and communication. Water scarcity is also very severe in rural areas. The condition of the Dalits and tribes is a struggle betweeen life and death as they are quite socially alienated.

The development has to be sustainable—as it should take care of the interest and well- being of the people, and also the ecological concerns. The biodiversity is to be kept undisturbed, so also the life of the subaltern people. Today's development programmes are by the corporates who tries to forcefully evacuate the Dalits, tribes/Adivasis, poor, and the fisherfolk from their habitat. In fact, the development programmes of the corporates and the governmental agencies are forcefully acquiring the land of the people and doing a big damage to the survival of the people.

The powerful forces are chasing away the powerless and forcefully acquiring the land and their resources. The forceful acquisition of land in Singur and Nandigram in the name of Special Economic Zone (SEZ) is one example of oppression. Another example is the K-Rail project of Kerala government. Without notice, and without compensation, even without proper sanction from the central government and ecological clearance, the Kerala government was trying to mark the land of the people with yellow concrete stumps. The government also tried to handle the protesters with iron fist. In the name of Vizhinjam (Trivandrum district, Kerala) harbour also the Adani Group and the Government of Kerala evacuated the fisherfolk from their habitat promising good shelter and employment opportunities. But they are not given any proper shelter so far, and many live in unhealthy living conditions, including the cement godowns.

The kind of oppression and exploitation in the name of development took place in Narmada Valley, and also in Niyamgiri (Odisha). There was forceful evacuation and the exploitation of natural resources. This is a deceptive agenda of the government and corporates that the powerless and marginated are to be made a victim of the development. Most of the development programmes are not people-friendly or eco-friendly rather they are the profiteering business of the powerful or dominant groups. The most victimized are the subaltern groups who are tortured by the dominant for their selfish interests. They even give false promises to the poor in order to acquire their habitat and to close them away.

The development should have a liberative dimension, and it should have contextual perspective and have to consider the grassroot experience. The micro-experiences of the people are to be taken into account in our concept of development, and it should aim at radically transform the lives of the people, especially the marginated.

(b) *The Perspectives on "Subaltern"*

"Subaltern" means people belonging to inferior rank. This term was used by Antonio Gramsci, the Italian Marxian thinker to refer the proletariat or the working class or labour class. Now we are using this term subaltern to refer the people who are marginated or victimized like the blacks, the Dalits, tribes/Adivasis, the poor and the victimized women. It can also include the slum-dwellers, the transgender communnity, and the specially-abled people. Most of the indigenous people in the world are also belonging to the subaltern, as they are oppressed and part of the lower strata of the society.

The most oppressed, the suffering and the victimized in the Indian context include the Dalits, tribes, the victimized women, the poor and the transgender community. The theory of exclusion is applied on these people who are the down-trodden. They are silenced and became voiceless. They are also the victims of the development programmes of the government and the corporates. The systemic violence of the dominant groups operated against them to dehumanize the subaltern. It is sad to say that we are living in a world where the poor and powerless have no hold.

The privileges are enjoyed by the powerful and the powerless are in utter inhumanity. Gayatri Chakravorty Spivak argues in her essay "Can the Subaltern Speak?" that the issue of the marginalized or the subalterns is that they are kept away from expressing their concerns and to involve in the policy matters as they are voiceless. Siding and speaking for the subalterns is a necessary task though it may be a daring and dangerous task. Graham K. Riach observes that one of the key point is Spivak's essay on subalterns (published in 1988) is that the world's poorest people have no voice in the society. She claims that the local elite-officials, educators, religious leaders and Western scholars can never speak faithfully for them, that is, the subalterns (*An Analysis of Gayatri Chakravorty Spivak's Can the Subaltern Speak?*, London: Macat International Ltd., 2017, p. 9). According to Riach, it is more significant to note that whether the subalterns can be heard? He observes that for Spivak there is epistemic violence as the accounts of history leave out subalterns (*Ibid.*, p. 11). Spivak argues that the subaltern women are doubly marginalized (first as the colonized and then again as women) states Riach (*Ibid.*).

According to Spivak, women are silenced by both colonialism and patriarchy, states Riach (*Ibid.*). According to Dipak Giri,

> "Etymologically the term "subaltern" is the compound of two Latin words—"sub" and "altern" where "sub" means below and "altern" means "every other". Thus, subaltern as a whole comprises all marginalized class of people—be it workers or peasants or women or any other person or group of inferior position irrespective of caste, class, ethnicity, age and gender." (*Subaltern Perspectives in Indian Context: Critical Responses*, edited by Dipak Giri, Chhattishgarah: Booksclinic Publishing, 2021, p. 1)

Dipak Giri continued to state,

> "Tracing-back history, though subaltern as a term was first used by the Italian activist Antonio Gramsci in his article "Notes on Italian History" which later appeared as a part of his celebrated book *Prison Notebooks* written between 1929 and 1935 referring to a person or group of people in a particular section of a society subjected to the hegemony of the ruling elite classes" (*Ibid.*, p. 1).

II. *Development and Its Impact on Subaltern Communities*

The developmental programmes are not for disturbing and damaging the life of the people, especially the powerless, but it should aim at the wholistic development of all people including the subalterns. Without considering the life's realities and concerns of the people, a proper development is not possible. It is very essential to be redeemed from the capitalist mode of development. We sometimes talk about the economic growth, but whether all sections of the people are benefitted from the economic growth of a country, or only few powerful or dominant sections are benefitted out it. It also has to consider the sharing of resources, and the public distribution system.

Development should have the goal of transformation. It has to transform the lives of the people. The social justice is integral to development, but that is mostly ignored by the authorities. John Desrochers begins his book *The Development Debate* pointing to the stark realities of life. He states that a few minutes walk on the streets of the cities confronts us with slum-dwellers, undernourished children, beggars, the unemployed and a variety of sick people (*The Development Debate*, Bangalore: Centre for Sociation Action, n.d., p. 3).

Since the Second World War, observing the hunger and misery of the people, the development became a key concept. Even before that the scientific, technological and industrial revolution had concentrated on growth and progress. In this concept of development, the misery of the common man is not the focus. In the industrial revolution more concentration was on the profiteering. It uses the labour force cheaply and there was exploitation. According to John Desrochers, "after the Second World War, the discovery of massive hunger, povery and underdevelopment attracted worldwide attention" (*Ibid.*, p. 6). General approaches are formulated such as socialistic, welfarism, modernization and so on, but the overambitious projects and approaches did not meet the goal. In Latin America also the developmentalism has failed, so the significance of liberation has come to the scene.

In many countries the UN agencies have funded for development projects and they are regulated by these forces. Most of these projects are run into severe corruption, and they did not meet the needs of the people. The funds came from IMF and World Bank are misused by the dominant groups of the Third World, and it did not cater the needs of the people. The subaltern groups became victims of some of the development projects, and never became the beneficiaries.

There are programmes by the government and other agencies to develop the downtrodden people, but it is so happened that they are not reaching the subaltern group of people. Rather, what is happening is very pathetic that they are oppressed and exploited. The public distribution system does not reach them, so also the infrastructure development. The socio-economic and political development of these people is only a distant dream. They are merely used as vote banks and there is no substantial development in the field of education, health care and employment.

In the name of development, the subalterns are forcefully evacuated from their original habitat. This was found also in the context of making dams (hydro projects), ports, mining and also developing Special Economic Zones (SEZs). The Dalits, tribes, women, fisherfolk and other victimized groups (transgender community, people with disabilities, slum-dwellers, etc.) are undergoing severe struggle in our context.

The fisherfolk are also forced to evacuate from their habitat in accordance with the ulterior motives of the corporates. It is for the development of corporates rather than the fisherfolk and other subaltern people. The recent Vizhinjam (Trivandrum) events are supporting this, as the Adani Group is making a seaport where the fisherfolk is forced to leave their place and no permanent arrangement is made for their shelter and employment. They live by the sea, and sea and seashore are life for them. The corporates are not sensitive to ecological concerns, the authorities are furnishing permission to there corporates disregarding the people and eco-concerns as they influence the political powers.

Unless there is an integral development in the life of the subaltern people, India cannot be developed. What is happening is the development of the elites than the poor and powerless. The infrastructure development as Dr A.P.J. Abdul Kalam suggested is to be introduced. It is "PURA"—providing urban facilities in the rural areas. There should be proper distribution of land and resources, concentrating on subaltern people. It is also importance to have employment generation. The shelter and food security are also very significant for their development. Poverty is a real issue in the Indian context as those who are below the poverty line may draw 20 or 25 rupees per day. Many of them have no permanent job, and a big number of people are bondslaves. The Indian caste system also does not permit the Dalits to have a social and economic mobility. The discriminative attitude of the dominant groups prevent the mobility of the subaltern people. The empowerment of the subaltern should be the goal of our development.

The globalization also leads to globalization of poverty and injustice. The free market economy is a fertile sphere where the capitalists and corporates could flourish by selling their products. Their intention is nothing but profiteering. By making attractive advertisements they sell their products, though they are not necessary or unwanted. They are found in the form of electronic goods, food items, pesticides, fertilizers, clothes, medicines and cosmetics. Their only intention is to tap the money, as the colonial forces were tapping the valuable resources of India. Now we see through the corporates the application of neo-colonial agenda.

III. *The Suggestions and Reflections*

The deceptive approach of the capitalistic agenda of the corporates is to be identified. What is the goal of development, and whose development are the important questions. The adequate approach should be people-oriented and it should consider the experiences of the people and has to start from the grassroot level. It should not be "top to bottom" approach, but "bottom to top" approach. It should start from below.

The pattern of development is found in the Nazareth Manifesto of Jesus (Luke 4:16-21). The marginalized are in the centre of his thinking, as they are to be empowered and emancipated. The last, least, and the lost should have the benefits of development and to be liberated. Liberating the subalterns from the clutches of the oppressive structures is the key to integral development. The social movements and social action groups play a vital role to resist the oppression against the marginalized as they organize and mobilize them.

Jesus and Jesus' movement was pro-poor and pro-subaltern and he was critical of the capitalist structures and the exploitation and oppressions prevail in the society. He was for the sharing of resources for the welfare, development and liberation of the powerless (Matthew 19:18-24; Luke 12:15-21). The early Christian community was also concerned of the poor and powerless (Acts of the Apostles 2:44-47; 4:32-35). They were willing to share their resources for the good of the poor.

In the Old Testament the Jubilee year (Lev. 25) was meant for restoration of the land and resources of the powerless. The prophets were against feudal structures which are oppressive and they stood for justice and had solidarity with the subaltern people. They challenged the unjust structures which prevented the development and liberation of the marginalized (Isaiah 10:1-2; Amos 5:11-13). If justice prevails everywhere as against exploitation, oppression and corruption, certainly the subalterns will have their development and liberation. There are programmes for development, but whether the benefits are realized by the subaltern people is the question. They are not properly channelized or distributed. The forces of corruption are there to hamper and to exploit the benefits of the poor and powerless.

At the time of pandemic also the rural and urban poor were greatly affected as they became jobless and there was no support from the government to conduct their daily affairs. The guest labourers, domestic workers and the labourer from different field were severly affected. But the dominant caste and class were stayed unaffected as they have money and control over resources. The packages that focused for the well-being of the poor and powerless in the budget was never materialized in their life. Our packages in the budget are only a paper tiger which are de-activated by the bureaucracy and the vested interested groups. It is so happened that whatever inclusive development we talk about have made the victimized more victimized, the powerless, more powerless. This would be very clear if we take stock of the condition of the subaltern people who live in ghettoes without any facilities and progress for centuries.

Concluding Remarks

Development is a fascinating word of the rich, powerful and dominant as they could grab the maximum benefits of the modern facilities of development. The questions of the poor and powerless are always neglected and the authorities make India flourish looking into overall growth rate. Many millions are away from their fake statistics and calculations. So what is important is to concentrate on the issues of the marginated when we discuss the question of development.

Chapter

2

Ethical Concerns in Psychotherapy/ Counselling

There are several issues involved in psychotherapy or in Christian counselling. There are manipulations and exploitations of different sort are found in this sphere. There can be the issues related to discrimination, sex and money, which are to be curtailed. Psychotherapist or counsellor has to be conscious of the people, the context and the issues.

I. Ethics, Psychology and Psychotherapy

Ethics is deived from the Greek word *ethos* which means customs, manners, habits or behaviour. It is concerned of guiding people in crises to take fitting or suitable decisions. It enables persons to make appropriate judgement by discerning the situation. The word "morality" is also related to ethics, as it is concerned of the moral behaviour. Morality is derived from the latin word *mos* or *mores* which means manners or behaviour. Morality of a person is very important over here. Ethics is concerned of the foundational aspect of systems and behaviour. Ethics is to regulate our behaviour and attitudes. According to Albert Camus, "A man without ethics is wild beast loosed upon the world".

Psychology is the study of mind and behaviour. Human behaviour is influenced by the heredity and environment. The genetic factors have a great influence on our behaviours. The chromosomal abnormalities also affect a person's behaviour. The present study of criminology and law are concerned of the context of person, so also the genetic factors. The instinctual factors are given importance by Sigmund Freud in his study on human behaviour. Kohlberg and Piaget have observed the psychology of children and found that the behaviour and rules are socio-centric. Ethics is quite related to psychology as both disciplines are concerned of human behaviour, attitudes and the responses to the issues.

Psychotherapy is derived from the Greek words *psyche* means "breath", "spirit", "soul" or "mind", and *therapia* means healing or medical treatment. While physiotherapy is concerned of the healing of body, the psychotherapy is concerned of the mind. According to B. Vinay, J. Lakshmi and Suresh Bada Math

> "Psychotherapy is a science which alleviates pain, suffering stress on anxiety Psychotherapy may also be used in combination with medicines to mental illness." ("The Ethical and Legal Issues in Psychotherapy", in *Ethical Issues in Counselling and Psychotherapy Practise,* edited by Poornima Bhola and Ahalya Raguram, Singapore: Springer Science and Business Media, 2016, p. 199)

The ethics and counselling are providing guidance and suggestions for the people in crises to take appropriate decisions of their own to overcome at the crises.

II. Ethical Approaches, Counselling and Context

There are different ethical discourses to address the issues from the context. The deontological approach is based on conventional wisdom, and it is rule-oriented or principle centred. The rules and principles are important, but the rigid rules without considering the context is not appropriate. The teleological ethical discourse is concerned of what is good and it is concerned on the goal and the progressive dimension. The deontological ethics is emphasizing what is right. The openness and taking into account the contextual realities is essential for a proper ethical decision-making.

The contextual approaches are considering the experience of the people and they emphasize the humanness (Paul Lehmann), responsibility (Richard Niebuhr, William Schweiker and Emmanuel Levinas). It is important to be sensitive to the world, and we are to participate in the humanizing activity of God. The "other" is also important as we are concerned of the people (the other) who are in crisis. The responsibility is also related to accountability and answerability. It is important to see what is the fitting response. The analysis, interpretation and evaluation of the data is significant to make a responsible response.

The liberative discourses are significant to redeem the people from their crises. In the context of challenges the integral liberation is essential to transform the people. The structural transformation is inevitable as structures of evil is contributing to several crises. The liberative approach is after the theory of inclusion and it rejects the theory of exclusion.

In the context of counselling, the enabling in the process of problem-solving is significant. The loving and humane approach is essential to help or to guide the people in the crises. The responsible and liberative approach is important to consider the questions of the people in a humane manner. Bringing what is good is the focus and goal. There are people in different crises like narcotic addiction, alcoholism, marital break up, anxiety, depression or psychological stress because of molestation or sexual assault. The systemic violence, our attitudes, misguided thinking, the pleasure seeking and evil desires can bring several crises to humanity.

Ethical absolutism also hinders people from taking a responsible and humane decision, so it is important to follow an evaluative approach, which is based on love, mercy and humanness, to guide, support, guide and to make a responsible decision in the crisis. An evaluative and contextual approach is open to the realities as it is not condemnatory but it realizes the crisis situation of the people and to provide guidance to overcome the crisis. Ethical absolutism is a rigid approach which is not sensitive to the context. But the contextual and evaluative approach is responsible and liberative which would help the people to redeem from the crisis situation.

III. Ethical Obligations of a Psychotherapist/Counsellor

According to Gerald D. Koocher and Patricia Keith-Spigel,

> "upholding ethical principles is an integral feature of successful career as a psychologist, social worker, counsellor, or other mental health practitioner". (*Ethics in Psychology and Mental Health Professions,* Oxford: OUP, 2016, p. 6).

The competence, integrity and responsibility are very important for any psychotherapist or counsellor. The informed consent from the client is a prerequisite so also respecting the privacy. It is also important to note that any person in a crisis is to be helped so there should not be any kind of discriminations in the name of colour, socio-economic status, gender and sex (LGBTIQA+) or sex worker. All people have their issues which need guidance and treatment.

The ethical principles put forward by Koocher and Keith-Spigel are important to be followed as the obligations are fulfilled.

1. **Do not harm:** It is the duty to help and care the client, and do not inflict any harm to them.
2. **Respect Autonomy:** Individuals have the right to decide how to live their lives as long as their actions do not interfere with the rights and welfare of others. Respect for autonomy is accepted by mental health professions, given that an underlying goal of psychotherapy and counselling is to move those with whom we work toward greater self-reliance and self-determination.
3. **Act Justly:** The actions of mental health professionals should be fair and equitable. Others should be treated as we would want to be treated under similar circumstances.
4. **Act Faithfully:** Issues of fidelity, loyalty, truthfulness and promise keeping converge to form the standards required in fiduciary relationships. The therapy relationship should allow clients to feel safe and as unencumbered as possible by irrelevant and extraneous variables.
5. **Accord Dignity:** Mental health professionals view those with whom we work as worthy of respect. We must strive to understand cultural diversity and ways others differ from ourselves and endeavour to eliminate biases influencing the quality of our service.
6. **Act Benevolently (Beneficence):** A paramount virtue in any mental health profession is to treat clients with

caring and compassion while maintaining appropriate professional roles and boundaries.

7. **Pursue Excellence:** Maintaining competence, doing our best, and taking pride in our work form the bases of quality mental health services.
8. **Act Accountably:** When errors have been made, mental health professionals consider possible consequences, accept responsibility for their actions and inactions, avoid shifting blame or making excuses, and take any available steps to minimize or undo harms and wrongs.
9. **Act Courageously:** Maintaining a steadfast determination to actively uphold ethical principles, including when we observe unethical actions perpetrated by colleagues and other rather than averting our eyes of fear of retaliation, is a challenging mandate. Those with true grit have an advantage in that courage itself emboldens us to do the right thing (*Ibid.,* pp. 1-7).

When dealing with a client as psychotherapist or counsellor, it is important to keep away or refrain from any sexual contact or other multiple role relationships with clients. Keeping the record of the consent of clients, and the details about diagnosis and the treatment or actions taken are important. The practise also should be within the paramaters of the competence of the therapist. With the consent of the client, referring the client to more competent counsellors if needed is also to be considered. The privacy or the confidentiality is to be maintained, and avoid any manipulations with lucrative goals (*Ibid.*, pp. 6-7).

IV. The Psychotherapist/Counsellor, the Select Groups and Ethical Issues

The integrity and moral sense is very significant for a

psychotherapist or counsellor as a practitioner. They are to provide guidance to different groups of people. The utmost aim is to bring healing to people. Here we are dealing only select groups.

1. *Children and Psychotherapy*

The children are undergoing several kinds of issues like depression, anxiety and attention deficiency syndrome. According to Vijaya Raman,

> "psychotherapy with children requires the knowledge of developmental issues, standard care practises, applicable laws as well as ethical principles" ("Ethical Issues in working with Children in the Consultation: Liaison Context" *Ethical Issues in Counselling and Psychotherapy Practise,* edited by Poornima Bhola and Ahalya Raguram, p. 58)

There are cerain guidelines as children are treated. They are as follows according to Vijaya Raman:

(a) Do not harm to the child.
(b) Do what is in the best interest of the child.
(c) Always strive to protect the privacy of the child's communications.
(d) Respect the child as well as the family regardless of race, religion, socio-economic status, education or intellectual level. (*Ibid.,* p. 58)

The crisis of the children are to be identified and providing guidance is crucial for the psychological development of the child. The characteristics of their stage (age-wise) is to be considered as we realize their crisis to guide them. They are always open and transparent.

2. *Couples, Families and Psychotherapy*

The ethical standards, values and guidelines are to be maintained as a therapist or counsellor deal with couples and families. The context and issues of the client are to be considered seriously as the clients may be representing multi-cultural, religious or socio-economic context.

According to Sobhana H., Priya Sexena and Buli Nag Daimari,

> "Ethical decision-making requires reflective awareness and sensitivity" ("Ethical Issues in Working with Couples and Families", in *Ethical Issues in Counselling and Psychotherapy Practise*, edited by Poornima Bhola and Ahalya Raguram, p. 88)

According to them, Gambrill and Strom Gottfried recommended the following factors to consider:

(a) The couples/families interests, rights and values.
(b) The interests and rights of others involved in the situation.
(c) Personal values and ethical stance, practise setting, policies and procedures the relate to the situation. (*Ibid.*, p. 88)

The competence of counsellor, keeping the confidentiality, integrity and responsibility are key elements to deal with couples and families. The practitioners should be accountable to the clients and they should be committed, just and fair in their dealing. Do not harm the well-being of the clients. (*Ibid.*, pp. 88-89)

In order to have an appropriate counselling, the counsellor should be aware of the cultural, religious, socio-economic and ethnic background of the client. The gender roles, the matriarchal or patriarchal system and also the practise of polygyny or polyandry in some communities are to be regarded in the attempt of psychotherapy. The families in India are going through the change of patterns. There are joint families, extended families and nuclear families. The issues are also complex in these situations. So it is important to be sensitive to the context in order to evolve a response to their issues. There are differences in relation to family as urban, rural, Dalit or even tribal. So the ethos and values may very divergent. Any kind of intervention would be made only by knowing throughly these factors. There may be situations of stalemate as the solution or decision-making is not possible, but the ethical mandate are to be informed in the context, though accepting or rejecting them are personal.

3. *Psychotherapy and Survivors of Sexual Violence*

According to Anuradha Kapoor and Chandana Baksi,

> "Violence against women is widespread and includes physical, sexual, psychological or emotional abuse and economic deprivation. Sex-selective abortions, female infanticide, sexual harassment, domestic violence, trafficking, violence due to sexual orientation, widowhood, old age, disability and HIV infection and rape during communal and caste conflicts are amongst the varied forms of violence women and girls face, both within their homes and outside." ("Working with Survivors of Sexual Violence: Ethical Issues and Dilemmas", *Ibid.*, p. 125).

The efforts should be made to advancing women's rights and ending violence against women. Swayam is a Kolkata-based organization is committed for it. It provides holistic support services ranging from counselling, psychotherapy, drop-in centres, legal advice, vocational training, employment and shelter to survivors and their children.

Swayam is aimed at encouraging women to move from being survivors to active agents of social change.

> "Swayam generates discussions and debate, advocates for change at the policy level, networks with organizations with similar goals, produces and shares information on women's right issues, compaigns and mobilizes public and state action to end violence against women." (*Ibid.*, p. 126)

The psychological and psychiatric help are to be rendered to the people who are affected. Swayam is understood as an organization believed in

> "transparency, social justice and equality. It adheres to the ethical principles of beneficence, fidelity, non-maleficence, autonomy, justice and societal interest in its work with women." (*Ibid.*, p. 127)

Conclusion

The ethical concerns play a very significant role in psychotherapy/counselling. The psycho-social problems are to be identified and providing adequate suggestions is an important task. The mission is to guide the people in crisis. It also may involve the praxiological dimensions like caring, equipping and rehabilitating the people who are in various crises. As Jesus had identified the issues of the people in the crises, and restoring and healing them, we are to involve in the holistic mission. An integral vision of mission is essential to help people to overcome the crises. The psychological, physical and socio-economic aspects of the people who are in crises are to be taken care in order to adequately respond to the issues. Ethics and psychotherapy/counselling have a dynamic complimentary role to play to address the issues of the people and to help overcoming their issues.

Chapter

3

A Christian Ethical Response to the Controversial Farmers Bill of India

The Farmers Bill was introduced and passed in the parliament by the BJP government (17 September 2020) which became a disturbing element to the formers of India, especially the farmers from Punjab and Haryana. The farmers started the protest on 26 November 2020 and it continued for a year (exacty 358 days). In the midst of the struggle around 719 farmers died affected by covid, the chill, suicide and by the Lakhimpur accident (deliberately running vehicles to the midst of the farmers). By 19 Novermber 2021, the Modi government declared that the Amendment Bills will be withdrawn as the parliament sessions start on 29 November 2021. The Prime Minister Shri Narendra Modi apologized to the people for the problem caused because of Farmers Bill, as the parliament sessions started. The problem of clarity and viability or relevancy of the laws are the important issues in this regard.

1. A Review of the Farmers Bills

The farmers of Punjab and Haryana camped in the Haryana borders, Tikri and Singhu. They arranged placed for their stay which includes toilets, library, shops and medical stores. The protest struggles were led by Rakesh Tikait. It is the longest farmers struggle took place in Indian soil for the rights of the farmers. It was a well organized struggle with strong determination. The strong will of the farmers ended in their victory.

There were three main laws in the Farmers Bill. They are as follows:

1. *The Farmer's Produce Trade and Commerce (Promotion and Facilitation) Bill, 2020*: This Bill was very much controversial so opposed. There is problem with business spheres and the business conditions. It considers the places outside the market also as business sphere. Those who has a PAN (Permanent Account Number) can involve in the trade. The farmers had the fear that this can help the corporates to control the business [*Malayala Manorama* (daily newspaper in Malayalam), 20 November 2021, p. 7].
2. *The Farmers (Empowerment and Protection) Agreement on Price Assurance and Farm Services Act,* 2020: It avoids the middlemen in the business of the agricultural products. The farmers can have direct contact with small scale and large scale sellers and exporters. It promotes digital selling and buying. The government assures the guarantee or assurance of price of the products. But there is ambiguity in how products are priced. If there is disagreement between contractor and farmers, there is no simple way to resolve the problem [*Malayala Manorama* (daily newspaper in Malayalam), 20 November 2021, p. 7].
3. *The Essential Commodities (Amendment Bill)*, 2020: The essential commodities bill was in force from 1955

> to avoid black marketing and hoarding. Here the new amendment has liberalized the conditions which can help the corporates to collect and store products without limit. The government control is minimal in this regard, which can help the corporates to have absolute control over the products. (*Ibid.*, p. 7)

Bharatiya Kisan Morcha is the leading organization behind the farmers protest, which is a common platform of Thirty-two organizations. According to Narendra Singh Tomar, the Union Minister of Agriculture,

> "these reforms keep in mind the long term interests of farmers. Though these laws, farmers have been given freedom to sell their produce anywhere in the country, and strike a deal even before sowing their crop, which will increase their income. The government also aims to increase production and productivity in agriculture so that farmers are prosperous." ["Reforms Look at Long-term Interests of Farmers" (interview with Narendra singh Tomar by Pratul Sharma, *The Week*, 20 December 2020, p. 45)].

The farmers were not happy with the new farmers laws, as they were not sure about the minimum support price of the produce. They had the apprehension that the prices may go down as the corporates take control of the markets. They had the fear that the market forces will regulate and control the prices of the crops. They depend mostly on the APMC (Agriculture Produce Market Committee) for their selling of products. They had a trust in APMC, which assures the minimum support price (MSP) and that will be undermined is the apprehension of the farmers.

Following are the observations on farmers law by the research of Pratual Sharma:

Highlights of the Farmer's Produce Trade and Commerce (Promotion and Facilitation) Act, 2020

Purpose

- Promote barrier-free interstate and intrastate trade in agricultural produce.
- Create additional trading opportunities outside the APMC markets.
- Help farmers get remunerative prices, as a result of alternative trading channels.
- Allow facilitative framework for electronic trading.

Apprehensions

- Market forces will decide prices of crops; MSP not assured, as it was in APMCs.
- Only helps corporates who want to enter the sector.
- Government may exist procurement, putting farmers at the mercy of the open market.
- Redressal mechanism not adequate; courts cannot be approached in case of disputes.

Highlights of the Farmers' (Empowerment and Protection) Agreement on Price Assurance and Farm Services Act, 2020

Purpose

- Provide for contract farming. Transfer risk of market unpredictability to the sponsor. Provide a national framework on farming agreements.

- Help farmers benefit from superior support mechanisms of corporates.
- Provide for mutually agreed remunerative prices.

Apprehensions

- Corporates can trap small farmers in exploitative legal contracts.
- Corporate to decide prices; MSP not guaranteed.

Highlights of the Essential Commodities (Amendment) Act, 2020

Purpose

- Remove fears private investors may have of excessive regulatory interference.
- Give freedom to produce, hold, move, distribute and supply crops.
- Help in harnessing economies of scale and attract the private sector into the sector.
- Help drive up investment in cold storages and modernization of food supply chains.

Apprehensions

- May allow big companies to manipulate prices by storing farm produce for longer.
- Consumer interests could play a larger role than that of a farmer.

Highlights of the proposed Electricity Amendment Bill, 2020

Purpose

- Ensure consumer centricity.

- Promote ease of doing business.
- Enhance sustainability; promote green power.
- Setting up a national committee for appointment of state regulatory commissions.

Apprehensions

- State subsidies in the power sector for farmers may be curtailed.
- Reduce state's role in power distribution.

Highlights of the Commission for Air Quality Management in National Capital Region and Adjoining Areas Ordinance, 2020

Purpose

- Control pollution in the NCR.
- Curb stubble burning.
- Impose penalties for violations—five years in jail, and fine up to Rs. 1 crore.

Apprehensions

- Will be used against the farmers who burn stubble.
- Farmers could be unable to arrange for disposing off stubble and pay fines. (*Ibid.*, p. 49)

The repealing of the farmers Bill is the only solution that farmers put foreward to end their struggle along with their families. After the struggle for independence, India must not have witnessed this form of struggle which is well organized and many families participated. The women were also in the forefront, so also the old people. Their fight with determination ended up in the repealing of the farmers Bills.

The international community also have shown their solidarity with the struggle of the farmers.

2. The Ethical Response to the Issue of Farmers

The government authorities or the powerful are always not concerned of the people and their aspirations. The political parties have their own ulterior motives. These factors may not be people friendly. The farmers are the backbone of any country, as their labour plays a vital role for the food security. Without the production of food, no one can survive meaningfully. Their diligent efforts are important in the area of food security, employment generation, the smooth functioning of markets, the reception of foreign money by exporting the crops, and the economic growth.

There is no Green Revolution without farmers. Millions are surviving with the agriculture. They suffer the loss in certain adverse situations. When fuel price, the price of fertilizers and pesticides go up, they are very much worried. They committed their whole life for the agriculture. They are after crops and the livestock. They live by that and also they let others to survive. Any kind of control by the government authorities and the centralization is quite deceptive for them, and they look up on them with suspicion. What they need is not big profits, but to sell their products with reasonable price and reasonable profit in accordance with their effort. They are not after or they have no time for litigations and appearing before the court for arguing their cases.

The farmers used to sell their products through *mandi*s (markets), which is collected by government agencies with a reasonable rate (rate decided by government considering their labour, the price of fertilizers, pesticides and the seed). This arrangement is overturned by the new Bill. The laws of farmers Bill are in favour of the corporates. It protects them and it is meant for their benefit and monopoly.

God is against the inhuman laws and the evil intentions of the powerful. The structures of domination are always oppressive and are against the people-friendly approach. Bible protest the dehumanizing rules and regulations. It challenges the injustices. There is divine judgement on the oppressive rulers (Jeremiah 22:1-5). God sides and has solidarity with the powerless (Amos 4:1-3). God is for justice and to empower the marginated (Amos 5:24). Like the prophets, Jesus was vehemently attacking the structures of oppression, which exclude the poor and marginalized. He was against the laws that were inhuman and oppressive (Matthew 12:1-8; 21:12-13; John 5:1-13).

It is important to question what is unjust and inhuman in the laws. The dictating of the law for the benefits of the powerful is a serious human right violation in India. It is also found in other Asian countries. This may be also a universal phenomenon. The laws are made by the powerful for the benefit of the powerful. This tendency has to be challenged. The farmers have their identity, dignity and rights. They should have an active participation in the decision making and the policies. The corrupt system also have hidden agenda which is radically challenged by the farmers of India, at last the government had to bow down as they repeal the farmers Bills.

The law should be the protector and guardian of the poor and powerless, but is abused and used against the poor by the authoritarian structures. In the Essential Commodities (Amendment) Act there is no control for the corporates to collect and to store cereals which will create scarcity of food products in the market, which will affect the public distribution system and it will lead to hike of prices. In the Farmer's Protection and Empowerment (Amendment) Bill, there is clause for contract farming which explains that the farmers have to agree to produce certain crops for the corporates for five years. The corporates can withdraw from the contract any time, and the farmers have no provision to file case against corporates. This can lead to severe economic problems to farmers. It also gives room for corporates to control the farmers and farming process.

There are several issues involved in the farmers Bill which will adversely affect the farmers. The Bills are not farmers-friendly, but corporates-friendly. A liberative approach is essential to respond to the issues. The principle of exclusion is found in the Bill as the farmers' aspirations are undermined. A radical challenge is inevitable to challenge the inhuman laws, as the rights of the farmers are questioned by the Bill. The pyramidal structures became the advocates of systemic violence, so a radical restructuring is essential. The struggles or protests have a very prophetic role which is liberative for the farmers. The organized efforts of the Indian farmers and their organizations were opting a very dynamic, praxis-centred approach which led to their victory-Jai Kisan.

3. Some Observations on Farmers Bill and Farmers Struggle

(a) The farmers are well orgaized and they had a determination to win their cause at any cost. They were willing to sacrifice even their lives for the cause of justice.

(b) The government machinery had attempted to foil the efforts of the farmers, but failed to suppress the struggle of the farmers.

(c) The unity of the farmers and their families and the solidarity of the people play important role which leads to the repealing of the controversial Bills.

(d) The farmers community constitute people from all gender, caste, class and religion, so they could consolidate the cooperation, and participation of all sections of people for their cause.

(e) It is a challenge to liberalized economic policies like free-market economy where the markets, especially the corporates control the products. The farmers protest is for their right on land and products.

Conclusion

The farmers protest was a historical event in the Indian context. They stood firm for the rights and just cause. Their commitment to soil and agriculture is also found in their struggle. The farm laws were found to be discriminatory and it is corporates-friendly, so they conscientized the farmers and the people and organized themselves to fight against them. The government machinery and their manipulations have thoroughly failed before the farmers determination. They did not want anything less than repealing the farmers Bills. At last the government or the authorities had to repeal the laws.

Chapter
4

War

A Deadly Enemy of Humanity

It is a tragice fact that the existence of war is found even in a civilized world. The world organizations like United Nations (UNO) have failed to control the war. The powerful countries are using Veto power to justify their own evil actions, and the world organizations stand helpless even as the powerful countries do tremendous amount of damage on the powerless countries. When Russia ravages Ukraine, the UNO or even NATO (North Atlantic Treaty Organization) were not able to intervene in the situation in a meanigful manner, but stood only as "paper tigers".

1. What is War?

War is a tension or conflict between two forces by which the deadly weapons are used over against the other to do cause damage. It is the show of power or strength. War begins from the rivalry and enmity, and the competition. One of the negative contribution of science and technology is inventing deadly weapons of mass destruction. The atom bombs and the nuclear bombs are the supreme examples for this.

Besides the different kinds of bombs, there are chemical or biological weapons. In the Second World War, the United States and the allies have bombed the Japanese cities Hiroshima and Nagasaki, by which millions are affected because of radiation. Many, including the children who are yet to born are badly affected by radiation. An apology to this deadly action is not an answer to the disaster.

The words of Bertrand Russel is very relevant as he said, the science and technology is meant for the good of the human beings, but now it has become demonic. The misuse of science and technology can cause suffering and death to millions of innocent people. According to Leo Tolstoy, the idea of war begins from the mind of the people. The selfish interests, competition and jealousy are the causes of war.

The religions also are at play in creating conflicts. The riots in the name of religious fundamentalism, the terrorism and also the crusades in world history have contributed to mass killing. War may be between two nations or so many nations involve in war as in the First World War and Second World War. There was war between North Korea and United States so also Iran–Iraq war. The war is now on between Russia and Ukraine. Russia was trying to invade Ukraine, and mass destruction is done. On 24 February 2022, Russian military had made an invasion to Ukraine without any prior information. Russia is not happy with the progress or development and their independent stance. The monopoly of Russia is being challenged by Ukraine and their leader Volodymyr Zelensky. Vladmir Putin, the Russian Premier is very arrogant and act like tyrant to destroy Ukraine. The buildings are destructed, so also the infrastructure. Many are killed by bombing and ran away for life as they find refuge in neighbouring countries. More than 20 lakh refugees from Ukraine are accomodated by Poland. The conflict between Israel and Hamas (Palestine) started in the month of November 2023, which affected thousands of people. Many are suffering including the children, and both parties had casualties. So many had to flee as refugees to other countries. Electricity, water supply, food, medicine and shelter are affected because of the war situation. Certainly in war, nobody wins but many innocents have to undergo suffering and death. Ware creates insecurity among the people.

2. War and the Consequences

War does not bring any good, but rather it brings what is bad and evil. War is not a solution to any problem, and it leads to destruction. War only brings damage in the social, economic, cultural and political life.

War does damage to political and social relationship between countries. The relationship and the idea of coexistence is always challenged by war. It creates fear, anxiety, security and tension rather than peace and harmony. The relationship between the conflicting countries are in loss of cordiality and cooperation. The unity of nations and people is lost because of war and conflict. Many people die, and became refugees as the consequence of war.

The economic life is also seriously damaged because of conflict and war. Millions of people are affected as there is shortage of food and they may have to flee from their houses leaving eveything for their safety. Large amount of money is also spent to accumulate weapons, which are used against the other in war situation within no time. The money which is to be spent for the welfare of the people are spent for war. War also destructs the buildings and other infrastructure like schools, hospitals and power plants. The economic loss cannot be easily calculated. War can only make the life of the people miserable. The smooth functioning of the social life is also affected because of war, so also the economic life. It badly affects the income-generation, employment and other means of survival. The economic structure of the countries which involve in war will be badly affected, and the people have to suffer even from extreme poverty.

War also damages the ecology. The bombing and the use of arms and ammunitions destroys the eco-system. It affects the biodiversity, the plant kingdom and animal kingdom. The atmosphere is also polluted because of war. There can be air, water, sound and soil pollution. There may be a vast amount of emission of carbon dioxide, carbon-monoxide, emission from chemical substances, also radiations. All countries who involve in war are in unhealthy competition to defeat humanity and the eco-system. The struggle for survival is a great task in the life-threatening situation.

The rich religio-cultural heritage of a country also is undergoing threat as the monument are being destroyed by war. The churches, the religious structures, the architectures, the sculptures and the libraries are affected by war. In the recklessness of war, all that is beautiful and valuable are destructed. It is a great loss to art and architecture. The war mongers are not aware of the significance of the art, history, culture and religion. The war can only destroy, and it cannot create anything new or good. In the war situation, there is a deliberate attempt to destroy what is religiously and culturally valuable and significant. In the Russia–Ukraine war also many structures which are monumental are destroyed by Russia. The Ukranians are also trying to cover up some of them to protect from the Russian attack.

3. Christian Perspective and Response to War

Christian understanding is against violence and war. War brings suffering to all people. War is against the harmonious coexistence of people, and the worst affected would be women and children. The women are also physically tortured and sexually exploited as they are caught as prisoners of war (POW).

The values of the Kingdom of God stand against the conflict, violence, disharmony and war. Kingdom of God promotes peace. Jesus asked us to be peace-makers (Mt. 5:9). War challenges the dialogical existence and the reconciliation and it involves violent and inhuman acts, so the values of the Kingdom stands apart from war. The teachings of Jesus was against enmity and it is rooted in love and peace. Peace-making is a humane act, as war is an inhuman act. It involves cruelties and inhumanity. The role of love, mercy and humanness are absent in war. According to Bible,

> "He (God) makes wars cease to the ends of the earth. He breaks the bow and shatters the spear; he burns the shields with fire." (Psalm 46:9)

War is caused by political rivalry which has social, economic and even ethnic overtones. War begins when one fails to accept and accommodate the other. When the sense is lost, any dangerous weapons can be used against the enemy which may even harm the whole world. It is evident that those who involve in war have given a least place to the sense, and a greater place to the ego. War is an arrogant attitude which involves invasion and mass destruction through massive explosions.

It is very important to keep tolerance to save the humanity. Any kind of provocation and encroachment will lead to war situation. So these are to be avoided. Fight is between the combatants, and not with the non-combatants. It is so happened that the civilians are mostly affected in the war situation. Killing the innocents is not the solution to the issue. In order to achieve their goal, any country and their military forces may involve in any cruel and inhuman act. So war is always deadly and demonic.

War became an international problem as countries are trying to defend themselves by the support of the other countries. The countries are competing to collect arms which are sophisticated in order to defend and to attack. In the arm race deterrence is one issue, and the other is to manifest their might over the other. The pacificism was very much promoted by the Christian groups like Anabaptists and Mennonites. Pacificism is one perspective, then there is just war theory also. It is to be noted that there is nothing just in war. War is dangerous and does serious damage to humanity and to the whole cosmos. The poor and marginalized are the most affected people in the war situation. Only severe damages can be done, and war will not bring any good to any country.

Conclusion

War is against the values of the kingdom. It can only bring dehumanizing effect. War brings fear, insecurity, food crisis, death, refugees, loss of property, pollutions, disease and wounds. It breaks the relationship and only breeds hate and disharmony. It creates internal crisis and international crisis. War challenges the value of life. War is not a solution to any problem. What is important to humanity is reconciliation, peace, love and harmony. The coexistence and pro-existence are significant, as Martin Heidegger has stated "we exist to coexist".

Chapter 5

Pseudo-Secular Forces and the India Question

The psudo-secular forces are attempting to the disturb the secular fabric of the country by introducing and applying the Hindutva ideology and trying to torture not only the minorities but also the people who oppose the fascism and religious fundamentalism. The fascist forces understood Mahatma Gandhi as the first one who opposed their agenda, so they shot him dead on 30 January 1948.

The Indian context is becoming very dark and worse as the fundamentalist forces are using all the subtle means to make India a Hindu nation based on their rigid Hindutva ideology. The demolition of Babri Masjid, the Godhra Carnage (Gujarat), the killing of the people in the name of cow slaughter and also attacking the Christian minorities accusing the conversion. A number of Christians and Christian ministers are detained and undergoing severe persecution as the Hindutva forces have filed fake cases against them misusing the Anti-conversion Bill.

The British Broadcasting Company has released the documentary "India: The Modi Question" in the month of January 2023, bringing the Godhra Carnage and some other issues including cow slaughter, the Citizens (Amendment) Bill and cancelling the special status of Jammu & Kashmir. Very calculating moves behind the Godhra Carnage in 2022 by which at least 1,000 people must have killed and many are tortured. The police, the administrative bodies and the judiciary were kept under pressure not to act when the violence against the minorities was going on.

When the Hindutva forces were withdrawing the special status of Kashmir also the police and military forces were used to suppress the commotions. The internet was interrupted, the leaders were detained and power was abused. When BBC was telecasting the documentary against Narendra Modi and the Hindutva government, though it was not legally banned, they used all measures to stop showing through social media and other digital platforms. They used force to stop showing the documentary which portray the torture and massacre of the minorities of India.

The democracy and secularism is in threat as there is intolerance, arrogance and exclusivism. The mono-culture and mono-religious attitude and ideology is a threat to democracy and secularism. The diversity and pluralism are not acceptable to the ideology of cultural nationalism promoted by Hindutva ideologies. They misinterpret the word "Hindu" in relation to India and the people who believe in Hindu religion. The word "Hindu" was never originally referred to religion, but a geographical area, that is, the people who live in the banks of the river Indus. The pseudo-secular forces are very clever in interpreting the idea of Hindu in an exclusive way and enforcing on people by creating a threatening situation as we see in fascism and Nazism. Their policy is nothing but annihilating the "other".

These fascism and exclusive attitude is also found in colonial forces. They also tried to annihilate the "other", the powerless. The minorities and those who holds the spirit of democracy, secularism and socialism are under hunt by the pseudo-secular forces. They use the maximum force to suppress their voices and activities. Religion is politicized and make it a shield to protect their interests and to realize their ulterior agenda.

The preamble of Indian constitution has the words like socialist, secular and democratic, now these words have no meaning in the Indian context as the pseudo-secular forces do not accept the plurality of religions and cultures. The significant question today is, what constitute India? There is an assumption, though it is not fully true, that India has 100 per cent tolerance to different religious traditions, but now we see that Hindutva forces are intolerant to other religious traditions, as they do not want to accept the diversity and pluralism. The country which had held the value to *ahimsa* (non-violence) is now turning to violence.

The Hindutva ideology apply the theory of exclusion against the religious minorities by denying the fact India is a country which constitute the Hindus, Muslims, Jainists, Buddhists, Sikhs, Christians and Parsees, the extreme form of Hindu Nationalism of the fascist forces undermine the secular fabric of the country. It creates a threatning situation. It can uproot the democracy and lead to inhuman rule says Manavendranadhan ("From Nehru to Modi" (Malayalam article) *Samakalika Malayalam* (weekly), 15 August 2023, p. 30). The Sangh Parivar is trying to demolish the ethos and fabric of the India, which is secular and democratic.

The fascist forces are attempting to rewrite the history, the textbooks, and even the constitution. They also try to make the bureaucracy including the judiciary saffron. This saffronization process is extending even to the social media by which they can obtain a public support. They want to extinguish the secular fire and to wipe out the bloggers, journalists or media persons and activists who have an anti-Hindutva or anti-fascist stand. The fascism is also found as they try to freeze the FCRA accounts of the institutions of the minorities. The hidden agenda of the fascist forces is also found in the Citizens (Amendment) Bill (CAB), in the cow-slaughter issue so also in the *ghar vapsi*. These are all the planned agenda towards a monolithic structure (one religion and one culture) based on Hindutva ideology.

The important India question today is whether living in our motherland is safe today? The life of the minorities in India is not safe. This is being proved by the Hindutva forces as they tried to induce and to implement National Register of Citizens (NRC) and Citizens (Amendment) Act (CAA). The concept of citizenship is also in danger. The fascist forces do not want to accept the identity, dignity and rights of the citizens who belong to the religious minorities. They want to delete the present provisions and clauses on citizenship and to add new clauses to support and to implement their subtle and exclusive intentions or agenda. Only the life of those who are accepting and supporting the Hindutva ideology is safe in India. This is a sorry scene.

The freedom of speech, the freedom to profess and propagate the religion, freedom to worship and the freedom to exist in this country are in question to the minorities and the secular forces. Our nationality is challenged by the pseudo-secular forces. The idea of coexistence and pro-existence are essential for a harmonious existence but they are in question. The anti-conversion Bills and the deceptive means and the fake allegations of the Sangh Parivar are playing a vital role in torturing the minotiries, secularists and humanists. The secular ideology, movements and the people are condemned by them as anti-nationals and terrorists. The print media and the electronic media are under surveillance and they try to control the social media by which they do not permit to reveal anything against the Hindutva forces.

India attained freedom by the organized struggles of all people who belong to different religious communities trusting that we all will live in this land without fear as our security and welfare is safeguarded. But what is happening in the opposite as the subaltern people are forcefully evacuated from their habitat, and the minorities are asked to leave the country as the citizenship is in jeopardy. What is written and accepted and adopted in the constitution are being nullified by them. They deliberately violate the spirit of the constitution.

Any theory or ideology that exclude the "other" (the subalterns or religious minorities or powerless) should not be affirmed or promoted as it is intolerant, exclusive, fascist, discriminative or prejudiced and dehumanizing. In India the proponents and supporters of Hindutva ideology try to apply the theory of exclusion rather than integration and coexistence in order to suppress and to wipe out the religious minorities and those who oppose the Sangh Parivar agenda of saffronization. When we say, "we people of India" it should not be those who follow Hindutva ideology alone, but people belonged to all religious communities and ideologies.

Conclusion

It is important to note that India has a centuries long history of tolerance and inclusion which should be upheld. The secular value of the constitution should not be undermined. The freedom of speech, freedom of religion (profess, propagate) and freedom of worship are integral to Indian constitution

(Articles 19, 25). If we ignore and reject the secular and socialistic values, it is disastrous. And now the "India Question" remains as a serious and complex issue.

Chapter 6

Communication and Social Media, Exclusivism and Fanaticism

It is so happened that all through the centuries, those who spoke against the powers and authorities are attacked and silenced. All over the world the media persons are attacked by fanatics. Though we claim about the progress, freedom in the sphere of communication (speech and publishing) and a civilized status, the exclusivism, fanaticism and intolerance are at the peak. Religions and ideologies are misused with selfish interests by the fascist groups.

Ideology and Function of Fanatics

Religion, ideologies, race and caste are used as a weapon or card to annihitate the other groups. Adolf Hitler was using the Nazi racist ideology against semitic race and other progressive movements which protest his violent and inhuman activities. The authorities try to make fake allegations and to imprison them in order that the protest can be suppressed by iron fist and disclosure of the fact can be snubbed. Hitler was censoring the print media of the time and denied the right to communicate. This is happening in most of the Communist countries. The rigid islamic countries also regulate the social media. The extreme fanatic element is found in Taliban. The right to express and communicate or publish is challenged by them.

The exclusivism is found in the period of Emergency at the time of Indira Gandhi. The media and journalists were on hunt and many are imprisoned because of their dissenting voice. They were not intimidated by the tyranny of the rulers. The black law were introduced to smash of the daring stance of the media persons and others who are progressive and socialistic. The strong protest and the mobilization of the people against the autocractic rule had led to the victory of the people.

Media does have a prophetic role in society as it stand against injustice. It is a corrective force. But it is so happened that the media is also hijacked by the forces of exclusivism and fanaticism. In India, the Hindutva forces are using social media for their support. They make use of print media, electronic media, digital platform and cyberspace for their own selfish agenda, that is to justify their exclusive and fanatic ideological stance. The freedom of the press is also in question as they would apply deceptive means to close them down. They are using the Enforcement Directorate and Central Bureau of Investigation for accomplishing their ulterior motives.

The raid of BBC (British Boradcasting Company) offices were begun on 14 February 2023 (Valentine Day) with a nickname "survey". The Income Tax Department enter into the offices of BBC in Bombay and Delhi. It is certainly the consequent revenge of the BBC telecast "India: The Modi Question". The Sangh Parivar agenda is to use the bureaucrats for implementing the Hindutva goal. As Hitler was brainwashing and threatening the officers to enforce the Nazi ideology here the Hindutva forces are using them to enforce their selfish and exclusive goals. According to M. Prasanth, the Sangh Parivar has already domesticated the national media, and they yield to Modi government. NDTV was also absorbed by the corporates like Adani who has friendship with Narendra Modi ("Now Onwards Foreign Media" [Malayaḷam article "Ini videsamadhyamangal" in *Deshabhimani* (news daily), 16 February 2023, p. 6]. If any media publish the criticism against Modi, there would be phone calls from the top officials to threaten them saying that there would be Income Tax raid and also no advertisement will be given by the government. They hunted down the media like Newsclick, Newslaundry and the Wire. They also jailed the people like the owner of "Alt News" Mohammed Subair, and to some they filed cases against them (*Ibid.*, p. 6). In the list prepared by the "Reporters without borders", out of 180 countries. India's position in relation to media freedom is only 150 (*Ibid.*, p. 6). Freedom of press and other media is in a real crisis in the Indian situation. Though India obtained freedom by their struggle to a socialistic, secular, democratic country, it has slipped into the hands of the religious fanatics.

The freedom of press, freedom of speech and freedom of media are integral to Indian constitution [Article 19:1(a)] but that is being challenged today. Speech includes communication through mouth, print media and electronic media but that is being challenged today. Media is to reveal the facts or realities without fear keeping utmost objectivity. The attempt of fanatic groups is to influence or otherwise to wipe out the media. Social media like Facebook, Twitter, Instagram, Whatsapp, YouTube, so also the print media in the form of newspapers and periodicals are playing a vital role to bring to light the facts. Today, it is so happened that the different groups are having their own media to propagate their views with self-interest. The objectivity and disinterest are being lost. So people now suspect the journalists and their reliability. In one of the surveys conducted by British Medical Association, it is revealed that the least reliable group is the journalists.

Indian secularism is in danger as the religious fanaticism is taking a brutal shape. The religious fundamentalists are uncritically romantic about the past. They are against diversity (they are for one religion, one culture, one ideology and one party), tolerance (*ahimsa*, non-violence) and inclusivism. The fanaticism also lead them to apply *shuddhi* (the re-conversion by force and allurement) and to persecute the minorities. The mass massacre in the State of Odisha (Kandamal) againt Christians is a blackspot in the history of independent India. The persecution is continuing in different states of India in the guise of anti-conversion.

The anti-semitic stance and the racial exclusivism and fanaticism leads to a genocide, killing around sixty lakh Jews through gas chambers and guilletines. The inhumanity has no limits as the tyranny rules the world. The Jewish holocaust was a black spot in the history. The people were caught and kept in unhygienic situations with a piece of bread and little water. No food is saved in some days and there was utter fear of death. Their pathetic condition was accompanied by fear, insecurity, hunger, stress and death. It was a death and life struggle and hope of survival is minimal. They were kept in a cage like situation where they could not move and shifted from one place to another (Victor E. Frankl, *Man's Search for Meaning*, London: Ridler, 2004, pp. 17ff.). The powerful fanatic group are playing with the life of others. It is certainly inhumanty, cruelty, torture and tyranny.

Another example of exclusivism and linguistic fanaticism was found in Sri Lanka. It was a Simhalese–Tamil conflict as the Tamils were massacred by bombing the Tamil occupied areas. Thousands of Tamils were killed and their houses and other were killed and their houses and other buildings were damaged. The aim of fanatics was to form as one people (ethnic group) one religion, one culture and one language. The Sri Lankan government had an exclusive approach as against inclusivism, diversity and pluralism. It was racism coupled with language, culture and religion. Animosity is the game of the fanatics and dictators over the powerless and minorities ethnically, religiously and linguistically. It was a genocide in Sri Lanka as it was an attempt to wipe out the Tamils who looked for their identity, dignity, rights or the empowerment and emergence.

The fanaticism of any kind is against coexistence and pro-existence. It brings only disharmony, disrust and hatred. The Taliban, the Islamic state and the Hindutva ideology are the vehicles of intolerance, arrogance and exclusivism. This fanatic attitude is also found among some extreme form of communism which does not permit the existence of the other. The Nazi ideology is another example as there is ideological fanaticism which challenges the other. These forms of distortions do prevail as they deny what is divine and what is human. The ego-centricity leads to any kind of despotic attitude which will end up in dehumanization, mass killing and anarchy. The fanatic attitude is also a denial of the "Image of God" in the other.

Accepting the other is a Christian attitude as Jesus said "love your neighbour as thyself" which is also found in the perspectives of postmodernism, post-colonialism and the liberation theologies and ethics which promotes the theory of inclusion and challenges the theory of exclusion. The fanaticism and exclusion are the contributions of insane mind and attitude.

The "Image of God" in us has to work properly, so also to accept the "Image of God" (Imago Dei) in others as it affirms the dignity of a person and also the indwelling of what is divine, the righteousness of God and holiness. It directs us to have an adequate self-understanding of ourselves and also the proper perspective on other person, which will enable us to evolve a community with Justice and humanness. The violence, exclusion and intolerance are inhuman. Freedom of speech or freedom of expression through different means is a divine gift which is curtailed by the fanatic groups. They use it for their own selfish interests and exclude others from exercising that right and divine gift. In the parliament the references against the Hindutva are removed from the records that is also an infringement on the right to speech. It is certain that the ideologies of Hitler and anti-Christ are in action in the Indian context today.

Chapter 7

Exploring Human Sexuality in the Context of Promiscuity

Human sexuality is a natural instinct and gift of God for physical fulfilment and procreation for the sustenance of humanity. Sexual behaviour is to controlled and regulated to be used in a responsible manner. Abuse of human sexuality is leading to sin and violence and it is manifested in the form of sexual manipulations and assaults. Human sex and sexuality are used in a promiscuous way as an instrument of entertainment, for lucrative purposes and to woo the people to get positions.

Sex tourism leads to the trafficking of girls and women and there is a severe abuse of sex as they are objectified. The women's body is reduced to be a commercial commodity. Many children are even brought to brothels by deceptive ways such as offering job and money, but they are to live in unhygenic conditions as slaves. The value of life is in question in this context. Child molestation, absconding, rape, killing after gang rape and sexual harassment are some of the issues in relation to sex and sexuality. Sexuality is an emotional state and sexual organ is to conduct the act of sex for sexual gratification or fulfilment. Human society has formed ethical norms and standards, but they are being violated. Now it is by the influence of secularization and relativism any sexual act has become permissive by consent.

It is so happened that the homosexuality and lesbianism are legalized by judiciary. The same sex relationship and cohabitation (living together) are now permitted. There is a serious question about what is "legal" and "illegal". There is a legitimization of what is understood to be illegal. The pre-marital and extra-marital sexual relationships are also highly relativized as there is a serious erosion of values. The religious authority and values are not given adequate importance by the society. Some religions are also keeping fluidity and ambiguity regarding sexuality. It is very significant to know that what is moral or ethical is ignored and people would like to act in an arbitrary manner.

The misuse of sex and sexuality is found not only among the common people, but it is also found among kings and queens, the politicians and the high officials. History is not merely the history of political events, but it is also history of the private life of many leaders who involved in irresponsible and illegal sexual acts. Not only the political figures, but some philosophers and literary figures also support the sexual promiscuity. The proper sexual act has to be carried out through the marital relationship which is a sane sex relationship.

The homosexual relationship with consent was permitted by the Supreme Court verdict on 6 September 2021 as they argued that Indian Penal Code 337 is against the constitution. So the homosexual relationship is legalized. It is to be noted that there is sexual exploitation and violence in the context of homosexuality and lesbianism. There is sexual abuse as young boys and girls are kept for their sexual satisfaction by the dominant people and this is a historical fact. The powerful can misuse the vulnerable and powerless in the context of sex. The bi-sexual relationships are also found common in the society as they are permitted and legitimized and these kinds of ethos can lead to sexual immorality and promiscuity. In the history, sex is used an instrument of entertainment and it is gained through money, power and different kinds of allurement which surpasses the divine purpose in relation to sex and sexuality. The abuse of sex is an objectification of human body and women are the most victimized.

Sex and sexuality are a sensitive and a hot issue as it is highly relativized and permissive. The polygamy and concubinage were also practised with an intent of sexual gratification, and this is found in form of polyandry and polygymy as monogamic sexual relationship is found insufficient. The lust towards sex is already a social problem which leads to promiscuous sexual activities and sexual assaults so it is very important to promote the sane sex relationship. It is very clear that any society upholds the sexual immorality leads to a decline.

Bible permits sex only in marital relationship and it is against incest, premarital and extramarital relationship, homosexuality and other forms of sexual distortions (Romans 1:24-27). There is an unholy nexus between sex abuse, corruption, alcoholism and narcotic addiction.

The sex scandals are also very common in the East and West. The political and spiritual leaders are also involved in sex scam. The human sex and sexuality are abused in a pleasure seeking world. The sex drive is a basic human instinct as Freudian psychology insists and its sanctity has to be safeguarded. There is tremendous amount of vested interests in the use and abuse of sex. The sanctity of sex and sanctity of marriage are given utmost importance by Bible. Theologically, the purpose of sexuality and marriage are for reproductivity and gratification within the legal partners. The male and female are created by God with this intention (Gen. 1:27-28). What is important is the accomplishment of divine plan than human. Sex and sexuality are divine gift which are to be used within the parameters of divine purpose.

The sex workers are involved in offering their body for the sexual gratification of others for money. They are forced or deceived or willingly choose because of poverty or found it as a lucrative way of making money. Many are found to be forced or deceived or because of extreme poverty. Sex tourism and running brothels are found to be a profiteering business, and commercial sexual workers (CSW) is now a legitimized business.

The question is whether we should promote this sex work? It is very crucial to find ways to rehabilitate them and to conscientize the people who involve in it. The sexual violence and dehumanized elements are behind this aspect, so also exploitation by the middlemen and brothel managers. They are taken and kept in unhygenic conditions and they are succumbed to many venereal diseases. The illegal trafficking of young girls with allurement is also a serious issue as it badly affects their education, health and future. There should have some remedies for the structural evils and problems.

Though there are rules regarding the prohibition of illegal trafficking of girls and women, these are not implemented in the proper way. It is very important to implement the rules that curb the oppressive elements as sexual violence is at the increase in the domestic situation and society. An awareness campaign is also necessary to conscientize the people on sex and sexuality. The values regarding the sexuality are to be emphasized rather than leaving the issue to fluidity and relativity. Arbitrarily dealing with matters regarding sex is very disastrous and it leads to gross immorality.

Chapter

8

Raj, British Raj and Democratic Raj

The rulers and their rules have positively or negatively impacted our life as a citizen of a country. From autocratic rule we moved to a so-called civilized system of rule. There was a movement from Raj to Democratic Raj. Once the native rules were ruling our country as they have their own kingdoms. Later on the colonizers including the Britishers have controlled our nation, and then comes the rule (Raj) of democracy. There shifts or movements are assumably for the good of the people (*praja*s).

Raj: The Native Kingdoms and Rajahs

For many centuries India was ruled by native rulers (*rajah*s) as it was divided into several small kingdoms. The Kushans, the Mauryas, Pandyas, Cheras and Cholas are some of the ruling groups in India. The Mughals also had a period of ruling in India. We had small kingdoms and small empires and there was constant fight between these native kings (*rajah*s). Their conquest is to loot wealth other kingdoms which are found in the form of land and resources (gold, silver, diamond and money).

They have also collected revenue in the form of taxes in order to fill the treasury. Part of the income is used for the administrative purposes and for the welfare of the people. The people had no right to demand anything from the kings or rulers. Any kind of insurrection is handled with iron fist. The bulk of the income is used to maintain the palace and to take care of the people who live by the palace. They are palace people. The kings, their wives relatives, the artists, the workers, and those who are in the court in the form of advisors to the king are the palace people. They live in pleasure and luxury. A huge amount of money is used from the common treasury to take care of them. When there no sufficient money in the treasury, the kings tried to overtax the people as the present day governments do.

There are issues like misuse of money, corruption and using the money for selfish interests. They also make buildings in the form of monuments to show their pomp and memory. By these rulers make the life of the people miserable. The people, usually, had a very pathetic life as the welfare of the people are not considered. Justice is denied if the kings were not benevolent and just. Most of them were like cruel masters. There was exploitation, inequality and injustice in all aspects of life. The *rajah*s were siding the powerful, and dominant caste and class grab all privileges and benefits. The ruling class did control everything and take the benefits like today's ruling political parties.

There was nepotism and discrimination. Most of the poor lived in extreme poverty as there was no meaningful survival for them. There was also forced labourer without proper wages. Slavery was practised so also sexual exploitation and oppressions of different sort. The powerless had no freedom to live with their dignity and rights. The rules and law are also highly prejudiced as there are rules for the powerful and rules for the powerless. Severe punishments were implemented on the poor and powerless. There was no proper public distribution systems and bulk of the produce go into the royal stock houses. The people are levied much from the agricultural and commercial activities.

The freedom was curtailed under the native things. The opinion of the king is supreme and there is no freedom of expression for the people. The totalitarian regimes today also practise the same fascist attitude. It is only imposing the taxes, rules and the decisions on the people by the princely administration. The favours can be received by the persons who support and praises to the king and lords. The powerful grab every benefit and leaves the powerless to utter poverty. This kind of attitude is found in today's context also. Every resource is for the powerful and the powerless are in severe struggle.

The British Raj

The colonial rule was also a tragic experience of the people. Most of the Third World countries were under the colonial rule as there is a saying "Britannia rules the waves". The colonialism has made every form of "development" for fulfilling their self-interest.

The Portughese, the French, the Dutch, the Danes and the British were competing each other to loot the resources of the colonized countries. The gold, minerals and spices were tapped by them and made the colonized countries a desert and native people end up in utter poverty. They have made airports, shipyards and railways to achieve the goals, that is for speedy transportation of commodities to their home country. They controlled the political administration and trying to oppress the people of the colonized countries. When they were chased away from the colonized countries, they entered the scenario with neo-liberal or neo-colonial programmes.

The colonizers had fought each other in India along with the continued fight with native kingdoms in order affirm their power in different geographical areas as they were wresling each other to build their fortress and to tap the resources. The Britishers and the East India Company were very successful in subduing the other colonizers and native kingdoms in order to facilitate their exploitation of resources. They applied the "divide and rule" policy and other deceptive means to achieve their goals. The military power was used to suppress the voices of the local people. The movements against oppressions and colonialism was controlled at the gunpoint. Many freedom fighters were killed. Several people of valour came forward to sacrifice their lives assuming that there would be a bright future for them especially the poor and marginalized or the powerless, but what happened was the opposite. The dominant class and caste were in control of power and they regulate everything to accomplish their vested interests. Still there is no hope for the common people even after the independence. B.R. Ambedkar was very sure that the Dalits will not have hope under British rule and in the post-British rule or after Independence.

Under the Colonial Raj or British Raj, the condition of the people was tragic and those who depended on Britishers were enjoying life. They lived in comfort zone. But the condition of the powerless was very pathetic. Those who are politically powerful are also usually economically power and realizing this fact the dominant groups try their maximum effort to usurp political power. It is also interesting to note that the corporates of the West and East are in collaboration to exploit the resources from the Third World. It is an unholy nexus in order to accumulate the wealth and resources. The most victimized of the agenda of the corporates is the subaltern people who are forcefully evacuated to acquire the land and to exploit the resources.

The Democratic Raj (The People's Raj)

The word "democracy" means rule of the people, that is the *raj* is already there in that term, but still the word *raj* used though it is duplication or repetition. When India became a republic in 26 January 1950, our country is a sovereign, socialistic, secular and democratic. We were looking for the independence to create a rule of the people or democracy but that is not the intention of the Sangh Parivar or Hindutva contingent. They want to shape India in line with the rigid and exclusive understanding of Hinduism, that is Hindutva, a fundamentalistic stance.

The hope of a nation was shattered as Mahatma Gandhi was assassinated by the Hindu fanatic groups to undermine the democratic *raj* and to establish a Hindutva *raj*. The political power went into the lands of the dominant groups and they were competing each other to avail the resources of this country. It is the *raj* (rule) of the Babus and Dadas of this country who are the landlords, businessmen and other corporates. Corruption has become the integral element Indian society, as Lord Action stated "power corrupts and absolute power corrupts absolutely". Those who are having income generating resources became politically powerful and they involved in corruption. The policies and programmes were set for their benefits and not for the poor and marginalized.

The expectation of the people and the dreams of the poor never came true in their life as the rich, the powerful and the bureaucracy have planned everything for their benefit. The structural evil prevail in our country in a severe from as there is inequality, injustices, discriminations oppressions and exploitations of different sort. The destiny of India under the native kingdoms, the British rule and under democracy is same since there is no hope for the subaltern people. The triple *raj* have only the same effect. Those who have power, wealth and deceptive strategies will be prospered and others will have the plight of dehumanized condition.

The powerful are trying to disempower others and they look forward only their own welfare, development, security and comfort. The live at the expense of the poor. The politicians have made promises to woo the votes of the poor. Charity is not a solution to poverty, but the structural change and equal distribution of resources. The condition of poor, Dalits, Adivasis and the subaltern women and children did not have much progress in the form of transformation or liberation. There is gross violence and human right violations against the powerless including the minorities. The Hindutva forces are offering promises to the poor and minorities to get the votes in order to achieve political power. It is interesting to note that they vote these forces believing their cheap and deceptive promises.

Since there is no sufficient educational and employment opportunities the people of India, especially the young generation is migrating to other countries seeking a bright future. Accumulation of wealth is the agenda of the powerful, the politicians and bureaucrats, and they are least concerned of the emancipation and progress of the poor and marginalized. The life of the Indian poor is in utter misery as there is no radical steps taken to uplift them. Our socio-economic structure is capital-intensive and not socialistic, and our "secularism" is a pseudo-secularism. The *sarvodaya* (the welfare of all) and *antyodaya* (welfare of the last and least) were the slogans of John Ruskin and Mahatma Gandhi, but our democratic *raj* has failed to accomplish that vision. The hope of the poor and our freedom and democracy was only a futile ambition, which has failed miserably to emancipate them. The real focus of democracy is thoroughly lost and failed in the Indian context, as the structure has become pro-rich than pro-poor.

Many people are pessimistic about the *raj* of democracy as they are not optimistic about the condition of the poor and marginalized in this evil socio-political structure. It was clear at the time of covid-19 pandemic that the poor were struggling as they had a life of "death", and the rich and powerful were enjoying life in a peaceful manner. The poor and powerless do suffer by the rule and structure and they are victimized. The inequalities and discriminations in the name of caste, gender and class continue in the Indian context. The power is transferred from the British Raj to the corporate of country and they ignore the poor and marginalized.

We can be optimistic only when we see that the poor and the subalterns are emerging in a radical way to the main stream of the society socially, economically and politically. India's development is certainly based on the empowerment of the subalterns. very deliberate and intentional goals and programmes are necessary to achieve this end. Then only we can say that India is socialistic. India is also secular only when the minorities are safeguarded. It is regret to say that what is taking place in India is not peoples *raj* but the *raj* (rule) of the powerful or elites and the corporates. The government machinery and rulers are found to be not responsible, accountable and answerable to the common people of India.

Chapter
9

Uniform Civil Code

A Critical Reflection

Few decades back in the wake of Shah Bano case, there was a debate on Sharia (Muslim Personal Law) and the need for Uniform Civil Code (UCC). In the religiously plural society, the legal action guide is a real problem. In a multireligious and cultural society people have different beliefs, convictions, rules or principles customs and practises. The different communities have their own particular practises in relation to ideologies, worship, marriage, divorce and succession. The practise of polygamy (polyandry and polygyny) are found among some tribal/Adivasi communities and religious communities. Polygamy (more correctly polygyny) is practised by some in Muslim community. It is an accepted practise, but all Muslim men are not practising it.

The divorce by saying triple "Talaq" is also an issue to Muslim women which leads to gender-inequality and insecurity. In the property rights also there is inequality as men have rights on property and women have no rights. This is also a discrimination in the succession act of Muslim Personal Law. Correction is needed for any community as there is inequality, injustices and inhumanity found in our existing laws, customs and practises. It is important to redeem the women and men from the patriarchal ideology which is dehumanizing. Any civilized society has to function on the basis of what is humane, just, fair or rightful and liberative.

In the context of marriage and divorce, the Special Marriage Act may be applied, but whether that is applicable to all communities is the question. Another major issue is that the Uniform Civil Code is a Hindutva agenda based on Hindutva ideology which does not provide room for divesity and pluralism. Hindutva is based on mono-religion, mono-culture, mono-language and mono-personal law. So Uniform Civil Code will certainly reflect the ideology and principle of Hindu fundamentalism. It is to be assumed that without changing the constitution, it is not possible, so the fundamentalist forces may try their level best to change the constitution, and by that they would delete the privilege for the minorities and insert the principles suiting to Hindutva ideology. And that would be dangerous and disastrous to the religious minorities of India. By their craftiness and power what all troubles they will make is yet to be known. It cannot be predicted now. They are also on the move to change Indian Penal Code, the Criminal Procedure Code, and Evidence Act.

Article 15(1) of the constitution states that the state shall not discriminate against any citizen on grounds of religion, race, caste, sex, place of birth or any of them. Article 25(a) provides freedom of religion—all persons are equally entitled to freedom of conscience, and the right to forcely profess, practise and propage religion. Article 51A(b) also suggests that it is the duty of the citizen of India to develop the scientific temper; humanism and the spirit of enquiry and reform. Article 51A(c) argues that it is important to renounce practises derogatory to women. So the significant fact is that any kind of arbitrary perspectives which harm or undermine the equality and justice are not accepted. So whatever law or custom which adversely affect the life of the people are to be reformed. It is not the liberty to justify any inhuman customs and laws. The overall ethos of the Constitution of India is humanistic.

Article 26(b) of the constitution has the provision for any section to manage its own affairs in matters of religion and Article 29(i) states that any section of citizens "having a distinct script or culture of its own have the right to continue the same". These provisions have to be considered when we discuss the Unified Civil Code or the Uniform Civil Code.

But whether these provisions would be considered, or the Hindutva agenda would be implemented is the question.

Though there is no unanimity over the issue of the Common or Uniform Civil Code among the different religious leaders, this idea is in the air. It is a controversial topic. While the Hindu religious leaders advocate for Uniform Civil Code, the Muslims and other minority communities are suspicious of it. Since there is different personal laws which conflict each other, the need for a Uniform Civil Code is being discussed today.

Each religious communities were permitted to follow its personal laws in the field of marriage, divorce, inheritance, succession, gift and adoption of children by the non-interference policy of British rules [Thomas Kadankavil, "Editorial", *The Journal of Dharma*, vol. XI, no. 3 (July-September 1986), p. 215].

Later most of the personal laws are accepted by the enactment of the Indian government. The question about the Uniform Civil Code came up in the Constituent Assembly of India soon after the Independence. According to Fr. Kadankavil,

> "The main supportive thought behind this thinking was that secularism clearly demands a Uniform Family Law, and that separate family laws for different communities would result in discrimination between the communities which is repugnant to the secular character of the state." (*Ibid.*, p. 215)

The debate over the issue of the Uniform Civil Code came out with the following clause which was adopted as Article 44 (Article 44 appears as "Directive Principles of State Policy", Part IV, Articles 36-50) in the Indian Constitution:

> "The State shall endeavour to secure for the citizens a Uniform Civil Code throughout the territory of India." (*Ibid.*, p. 215).

The "Directive Principles" were not conceived to be mandatory. According to Fr. Thomas Kadankavil,

> "If the directive concerning the Uniform Civil Code is made mandatory, it would go against the following fundamental right enunciated in Article 25: subject to public order, morality and health and to other provisions of this part, all persons are equally entitled to freedom of this part, all persons are equally entitled to freedom of conscience and the right to freely profess, practise and propagate religion." (*Ibid.*, p. 216)

Tahir Mohmood is suspicious of those who advocate for Uniform Civil Code. He states,

> "The slogan of a Uniform Civil Code seems to have been adopted by as a camouflage to attempt

> wiping off the cultural traditions of all the religious minorties in India." [Tahir Mohmood, Uniform vs. Common Civil Code in India", *The Journal of Dharma*, vol. XI, no. 3 (July-September 1986), p. 228]

According to S.N. Balasundaram:

> "The desire for a common civil code in India is a thurst towards modernity in traditional society which seeks to weld the mutually exclusive communal and religious groups into a united and viable society. It is a laudable but difficult to attempt at laying the foundations of secularism which is envisaged by our constitution and, in the context of a religiously pluralistic society means an equal respect to all religions, though thus is not the meaning in which Westerners understand the concept." [S.N. Balasundaram, "The Conflict between Tradition and Modernity", *The Journal of Dharma*, vol. XI, no. 3 (July-September 1986), p. 230]

Balasundaram sees the positive elements of a Uniform Civil Code as he states,

> "By fostering the secular democratic values of liberty, equality and fraternity which form the ideological basis of our constitution, we can build an integrated nation. One of the practical means of strengthening the bond of political unity between the different religious communities is to lay the firm base for an integrated Indian society. It is in this context that the framing of a common civil code assumes

> great significance. For such a code reflecting the secular spirit of the constitution would strengthen the existing social bonds and foster the political integration of the different religious communities by subjecting them to a common judicial procedure in respect of the personal law." (*Ibid.*, pp. 237-38)

Though the discussion over the Uniform Civil Code is there, it is difficult to come to the agreement on how to do that in religiously and ethical pluralistic society. The Hindus, the Jainists, Buddhists, Muhammadans, Sikhs, Parsees and Christians have their culture, the values and perspectives on the issues like sexuality and marriage. Unless religious leaders come to certain common understand it is not easy. Though Tahir Mohmood accepts that the Special Marriage Act of 1954 is understood as step towards Common Civil Code, there is no one presented a concrete picture of the form and contents of the proposed code. [S. Tahir Mohmood, "Uniform Civil Code and Islamic Law", *Religion and Society*, vol. XXVI, no. 4 (December 1979), pp. 29, 36]

Asgar Ali Engineer talks about the moulding of Hindu customs so also the Muslim. The reform of the Muslim Personal Law is desirable in his view. In order to do that we should avoid the terms "change" or "reform" but use the phrase "creative interpretation in the changed context, [Asgar Ali Engineer, "Uniform Civil Code and Indian Muslims", *Religion and Society*, vol. XXIV, no. 4 (December 1979), p. 84].

Asgar Ali Engineer's observation should be noted that it is important to reform the personal laws of different religious communities. This is applicable to Christian Personal Law also. The prejudice against the women should be avoided from the Christian Personal Law. It is necessary to make a "creative interpretation" of the religious texts in the changed context, in order to make the texts and its principles or teachings relevant to the particular community and the community at large.

Instituting certain common norms and principles based on love, justice, equality and humanness is important in any ethically plural context. This can be applied to Indian context also. Asgar Ali Engineer rightly states,

> "India is a secular nation and as such has to serve all her citizens irrespective of caste or religion on an equal basis and ensuring them all universally accepted human rights. This applies as well to the domain of conjugal relations, inheritance etc. as to any other social or political domain." (*Ibid.*, p. 80).

But whether these provisions would be considered, or the Hindutva agenda would be implemented is the question.

A nation-wide discussion with the participation all sections of peoples (the experts of the constitution and law, the religious leaders, the political leaders and the intelligentsia (scholar from different disciplines) are necessary to come to an agreement on this issue of unified law for this country which is known as Uniform Civil Code. Suggestions for the factors to be considered in the Unified Civil Code.

(a) Consider the people and their cultural and religious diversity/pluralism—their particular belief and practises.
(b) Willingness to challenge and modify practises that are unfair, inhuman and ineqalities of different sort which affects badly the men, women and children.
(c) Do not try to impose the Hindutva agenda in this regard as India is a democratic, secular and socialistic country.

It is important to note that if the authorities are imposing a particular civil code on people without gathering the confidence of the people, especially the religious minorities it may lead to disharmony and trouble. The ethical consciousness, the sensitivity, integrity and sense of humanness is essential to evolve an adequate Uniform Civil Code.

Chapter

10

The Manipur Crisis

A Black Spot in the History of the Independent India

There was an ongoing struggle among tribals and non-tribals (Kukis and Meiteis) in the State of Manipur. That struggle has exploded in the form of a severe conflict between the Kuki tribe and the Meiteis. It created a war-like situation in a small state of India. The sorry scene is that very sophisticated arms and ammunitions are used in the fight. It started as an ethnic conflict and it combined the religious factors. The Kukis have understood it as an attempt of genocide or state-sponsored ethnic cleansing. It is also certainly an attack on minorities, especially the Christians. The most dangerous fact was that though there are several kinds of atrocities done on the powerless minorities, the rulers including the prime minister of India was keeping silent on this issue and failed to intervene in the situation.

The government authorities had to awake from the sleep only when the Supreme Court had intervened in the situation and condemned the assault on women as inhuman, cruel, violation of human rights and a shame to a country where there is a prevalence of democracy and constitution. Those who are supposed to support the subalterns and minorities have given a silent support to continue the atrocities on them. In a secular country like India, the Hindutva ideology and the agenda of Sangh Parivar is a curse as they are fascist. This fascist ideology was applied in the context of Manipur, as in Godhra Carnage in Gujarat. Life of a citizen is unprotected so the survival in India is a crucial issue. If the Hindutva prevails in India, it will certainly lead to the annihilation of the minorities. The fascist ideology always supports the violence and the annihilation of the other. The Sanatana Dharma and the concepts like *ahimsa* (non-violence) and *karuna* (mercy) and *shanti* (peace, harmony and reconciliation) are made neutralized by these fascist forces. The so called Sanatana Dharma (the universal law of harmony) is never practised in the Indian context.

In the month of May 2023 (3 May) the issue began in the wake of the comment asked the Manipur government in the month of April by the High Court of Manipur to consider Scheduled Tribes privilege to Meiteis, which was a privilege of the tribal communities. In this context, the Kukis had the tribal solidarity March. The Meiteis who are the majority of the population (more than 60%) and they live in the valleys and tribal people in the hilly areas. The hilly areas are a protected area for the tribes, and tribal people only can occupy and make transactions on land. When the Meiteis becomes Scheduled Tribes, they can also occupy and buy these lands which are reserved for tribes, and this has made a panic, threatening and insecure situation among tribal people in Manipur.

The tribal people had a rally on 3 May in Churchandpur to protest against this move of the High Court which had led to the clashes between the Kuki community and Meiteis community. The Meiteis on the next day entered the Kuki villages with arms and ammunitions and started burning their houses, worship places, schools and hospitals and killed their men and women and children. The sad fact is that they raped the Kuki women and tortured them, and it is reported from Kangpoi district that two women were paraded naked and gangraped. It took place on 4 May. It is reported that 200 Kuki villages were set ablaze and more than 60,000 people displaced. Around 200 people involved in the gangrape. It is found that twenty-seven tribal women were killed in Manipur. Out of twenty-seven, seven women were sexually assaulted or raped, and eleven women were beaten to death, five women were shot dead, two women were burnt. Several tribal men were also killed in the context of the ethnic tension in Manipur.

There are around 160 people were killed in the conflict, 300 churches and 5,000 houses were burned or demolished and even there is cases of beheading and chopping the bodies into pieces. They also demolished theological colleges and other institutions. There is a suspension or ban on Internet which also affected the life of the people as the right to information was curtailed. Most of the reports received only after seventy-seven days. The government authorities were adding oil on the fire by suspending the Internet which was an infringement on human rights. According to Sashi Tharoor, it disrupts the normal life and disempower people.

Now, the Kukis do not want to live with the Meiteis and they feel insecure and unprotected. They argue for a separate geographical area (statehood). They look forward the allotment of a separate Kuki area—the central government has failed to intervene in the situation when the High Court has made a suggestion to consider the Scheduled Tribes provilege to Meiteis, which was a constitutional issue that is to be dealt by the upper bodies of India (e.g. Supreme Court and parliament). The authorities have failed to take care in dealing with a sensitive and high voltage issue which has led to burning, lynching, torturing, sexual assault, killing and massive violence.

In the context of human right violation, justice has to be done to the tribal people in Manipur. Peace-talks only can lead to reconciliation and harmony. The restoration of tribal habitation (their villages, houses, worship places, hospitals and schools) is essential and also the provision of the compensation to the victimized. It is important to change the agenda of Sangh Parivar to name some group of Indian citizens as aliens, non-Indians and non-citizens. It is a clever device of Hindutva ideology to wipe them out from their own country.

It is important to control the riots as it has an ulterior motive of acquiring the land and resources of the Kukis by the Meiteis. The silence is a crime in the context of cruelty and inhumanity. Siding and having solidarity with the powerless and victimized and their causes is human and Christian. The life of a human being and a citizen of India is valuable whether they belong to Kuki or Meitei or any other ethnic group as they have the rights and privileges which are found in the Indian constitution and the universal declaration of the human rights. The identity, dignity and rights of all human beings are to be safeguarded and that is the responsibility of nation. Any kind of inhumanity, cruelty and brutality cannot be tolerated. What is happening in Manipur is a black spot in the independent India. Ramachandra Guha opined that it is a failure of the government in the national crisis. Like the black organization "black lives matter" the slogan of the tribal women and men in Manipur is "tribal lives matter".

Chapter
11

The Principle "Dharma" in the Indian Context

Dharma is considered to be a very significant principle in Indian context. It is very much found in Indian religious literature. In Pali it is *dhamma* which is found in Buddhist literature. *Dharma* means duty, and it comes from the sanskrit *dhr* which indicates "upholding" or "sustaining". It is also related to the word *rita* (*rta*) which means order and harmony.

The duty of the kshatriya is to wage war, so Krishna was telling Arjuna (who was in a moral dilemma to kill his relatives) to use his craft of archery against the relatives who are supposed to be the opponents as it is the duty of a kshatriya. The *chaturvarna* (fourfold caste) is based on different duties—brahmana has prietstly duties, kshatriya to wage war, the vaishya to involve in commerce and shudra, the service. Of course, *panchamas* or outcaste (the so-called untouchables) are not included in the four castes, and they are supposed to do menial jobs. This concept is introduced by the Aryans in India and they must have received this idea from Mediterranean religion. The Brahmanic forces were using this principle in a deceptive manner to degrade dehumanize and to oppress the Dravidian race.

This principles of *dharma* is found in Vedas, Upanishads, Ithihasas (epics) and Shasthras (the books on ethics and morality). Some of the neo-Hindu thinkers tried to relate caste as class. Caste is social and ritual ranking, and class is economic ranking, so these concepts are totally different. In the name of duties (*dharma*) the people are graded as inferior and superior. The Brahmanic forces introduced this pyramidal structure to affirm their hegemony over others. They have made the shudras and *panchamas* as inferior and disempowered them, and *panchamas* are considered as polluted. The so-called low castes are forced to do the cleaning works, disposing carcasses and other menial jobs and the pollution is ascribed on them.

The dharmic principle is not merely based on duties, but it is integrally related to caste system (*chaturvana*) and divided the people as "pure" and "impure". People in India are born to a particular caste and on that basis the *dharma* (duties) prescribed. This practise is known as *kuladharma* (caste duties). No one is supposed to evade the *kuladharma* as it is imposed on them. The people belonging to inferior castes are also mostly the bond slaves to the upper caste people.

There are also personal duties which is known as *svadharma*. So also the *sadharana dharma*, the ordinary duties. The common duties and responsibilities are there for all human beings and imposing certain duties by categorizing the people is an assault on identity, dignity and rights. The danger is the categorization of "pure" and "impure" (caste) and dignified and non-dignified (duties). Caste is a distinctive principle found in India which degrades, dehumanize and divides the people.

There is also the so-called "Sanatana Dharma", the universal or unchangeable duties and principles. It is a term later introduced in order to affirm the beliefs, duties and practises based on religion (*dharma*). The *ahimsa* (non-violence, tolerance), *shanti* (peace and harmony), *karuna* (mercy, compassion), love and brotherhood may be the fundamental and eternal laws. Recently there is controversy over the Sanatana Dharma. Sanatana Dharma is a consolidation of principles and practises from Hindu religious scriptures, and it is important to note that it is never practised in the Indian context as there is violence, including systemic violence in the name of caste and religion. If *ahimsa*, mercy and love are part of Sanatana Dharma, it is never practised in Indian context and as there is violence against the Dalits ad other powerless by the dominant groups.

The Indian Hindu religious scriptures affirm only the caste system and these scriptures never affirm the equality. The caste system or *chaturvana* is supported by *Rigveda*, *Bhagavata Purana*, *Manusmriti*, Upanishads and epics. *Bhagavad Gita* also advocates for caste system (4:13). The Sanatana Dharma never exists in India, as there is no concept of equality, states T.S. Shyam Kumar. He argues that there is no value system in Hinduism which is unrelated to caste system. In his view the *varnashrama dharma* and *karma-samsara* are so related. Caste system is integral to *karma-samsara*, and it is also important to note that there is no *sayujya* or *moksha* (liberation) for *panchamas* or the so-called low caste people.

Syam Kumar is critical of the statement of Swami Vivekananda that Kerala was lunatic asylum as he saw the influence of the caste system in the whole Indian context. He states that in Bengal also caste system was prevalent, so also all over India. Vivekananda's comment should be, he states, applicable to the whole of India. B.R. Ambedkar was very conscious that the Hindu scriptures are permeated by caste system, so he reolved that there is no Hindu religion without caste. It is true that Hinduism cannot exist without caste system, as it is integral to Hindu religion.

Gandhiji was critical of untouchability but he never attacked the caste system as he believed that it is a necessary social order, and it is like class system. He was very conscious of the fact that there is no Hinduism without caste. It should be kept in mind that Sanatana Dharma cannot exist as long as caste exist, as Sanatana Dharma, caste and Hindu religion are integrally related. If caste system is a violent dehumanizing principle, how the Sanatana Dharma exist? It is true that no Hindu scriptures affirm equality and fraternity, but only Indian constitution as it affirms the humanity and rights of all people.

The Indian context is socially stratified into different castes. There are four main castes so also the fifth caste, the *panchamas* (outcastes). The Hindu religious literature starting from the Vedas approve the *varna* theory—*savarna* and *avarna.*

The Indian societal life as based on the caste-duties. Particular duties are ascribed to certain castes. It is known as *kuladharma*—based on our birth (birth in particular caste group).

Caste system is the cancer of the Indian society and it is the most dehumanized system to degrade and discriminate and marginalize people.

- The caste system is a means used by the upper castes to exploit and to oppress others.
- The *Rigveda*, the Upanishads and *Manusmriti* so also the epics have given a clear indication about the caste system. The people with dark complexion are referred as *dasas* (servants).

- *Dharma* is a traditional order in the society which includes different duties which are social and religious.
- In Hinduism there is *svadharma* (duties of individuals) *kuladharma* (caste duties), *sadharana dharma* (ordinary or common duties) and *sanatana dharma* (duties which have universal value).
- Indian social situation and system is having the complexity of castes and sub-castes.
- There is gradation in status, and there are differences in occupation, food habits, dress, rituals and practises and way of life according to caste system.
- Caste system keeps people in water-tight compartments which prevent social mobility to the subaltern people.
- Chanakya's or Kautlya's *Arthshastra* (400-300 BCE) also asserts the superiority of priestly class. He was a supporter of Brahmanic class.
- The pollution and untouchability are ascribed on the Dalits in the name of caste.
- The caste and Christ will not go together. It is certain that the Christian values are totally against caste system, which is dehumanizing practise. Jainism and Buddhism have challenged the caste system to an extent. But Christianity and Christian missions have worked for the social transformation and liberation. This structural evil was challenged by Tranquebar Mission, Serampore Mission, L.M.S., C.M.S and Basel Mission.
- The humanistic trends, secularization and the urbanization also have contributed to reduce the importance of caste and its evils.

Chapter
12

Conclusion

There are several issues that people confront in the Indian context in the form of corruption, forceful evacuation of the powerless and also the reckless development. The issue of the subaltern people are unanswered by the political authorities. They also evolve laws and regulations disregarding the issues of the people. One such law was the Farmers (Amendment) Bill which was an utter failure. The pseudo-secular forces are trying to control the power and the media, and they are reduced to be exclusive and fanatic which is a great threat to the secular fabric of our country. The sexual promisecuity is another issue that undermines the concept of sanctity in sex and family. The Uniform Civil Code is also an agenda of the pseudo-secular forces with certain ulterior motives. The Manipur ethnic crisis is a black spot in Indian history as the tribal people suffer several sorts of assaults from the dominant groups, and the government machinery was failed to control the situation.

The ethical concerns are raised also in the context of psychotherapy, and also the war situation. War is an inhuman activity. The principle of *dharma* is used to subjugate and enslave the Dalits and other powerless people. A critical look into the Indian and the wider context is necessary to explore the real issues of the people and to form an adequate social order where there is humanity and the empowerment of the poor.

Bibliography

Barreto, Duarte (n.d.). *India's Search for Development and Social Justice*, II: *The Indian Situation*, Bangalore: Centre for Social Action.

Deogaonkar, S.G. (1994). *Tribal Administration and Development*, New Delhi: Concept Publishing Company Pvt. Ltd.

Desrochers, John (n.d.). *India's Search for Development and Social Justice*, I: *Development Debate*, Bangalore: Centre for Social Action.

Dreze, Jean and Amartya Sen (2013). *An Uncertain Glory: India and Its Contradictions,* London: Penguin Books.

Gaikwad, Roger and Thomas Ninan (ed.) (2017). *A Theological Reader on Human Sexuality and Gender Diversities: Envisioning Inclusivity*, Delhi: ISPCK.

Habib, Irfan (2001). *The Economic History of Medieval India: A Survey*, New Delhi: Tulika.

Kuruvilla, Philip (ed.) (2017). *Christian Response to Issues of Human Sexuality and Gender Diversity: A Guide to the Churches in India*, Delhi: ISPCK.

Maharajan, M. (1998). *Economic Thought of Mahatma Gandhi*, New Delhi: Discovery Publishing House.

Riach, Graham K. (2017). *An Analysis of Gayatri Chakraborty Spivak's can be Subaltern Speak?*, London: Macat International Ltd.

Index